Duck Feet

By Alan Trussell-Cullen

Illustrated by Boris Silvestri

Chapter 1

Tony's Big Feet

Tony had big feet – really big feet! His feet were so big, they just didn't seem to belong to him.

Tony hated his big feet. He hated going to the shop for new sneakers because the man in the shop always made a joke about his big feet.

Sometimes his friends made jokes about his big feet too.

But Barney White was different. He was the biggest kid in Tony's class, and the meanest. He was always being mean to Tony. He used to call him 'Duck Feet', and say things like, "Look out! Here comes Duck Feet! Be careful he doesn't stand on you! He'll squash you like a bug!"

Tony asked his parents what he should do about his big feet. They just smiled and said that his feet weren't all that big.

"But Barney White calls me Duck Feet!" said Tony.

"Look him in the eye and tell him not to be mean!" said Mum.

"But he's bigger than me," said Tony.

"Mmm," said Dad. That's what he always said when he was thinking.

Chapter 2

Dad's Great Plan

On the first morning of the school holidays, Tony's dad woke him early. "Come on," he said. "We have to be down at the swimming pool by seven o'clock."

"What for?" said Tony.

"Swimming lessons!" said Dad. "It's time you put those big feet of yours to work."

The first thing the swimming coach said when she saw Tony was: "Great feet!"

Tony looked down. "Some of the kids call me Duck Feet!" he said.

"Ducks are great swimmers," said the coach. "With feet like that, you could be a great swimmer too."

Every morning, all through the holidays, Tony went with his dad to the swimming pool. The coach soon had Tony kicking properly, and he was beginning to swim faster and faster.

Chapter 3

A Surprise for Mr Cool!

Soon it was time to go back to school. Tony was looking forward to seeing his friends again. But as he walked into the classroom, the first person he saw was Barney White.

“Here comes Duck Feet!” Barney shouted. “Where were you in the holidays? I didn’t see you around.”

“I was at home,” Tony said.

He didn’t say anything more than that. The last person he wanted to know about his swimming lessons was Barney White!

"I know where he was," said Tony's friend Mandy.

Mandy had taken early morning swimming lessons too. Tony shook his head at her, but she wasn't looking at him.

"He was down at the pool having swimming lessons!" she said.

"What?" laughed Barney, pointing at Tony's feet. "You mean he can swim with those two big anchors?"

"He can swim very well!" replied Mandy. "In fact, I think he can swim so fast, he'll beat you at the school's big swimming race!"

"Wait a minute!" said Tony. "I'm not swimming in the big race!"

"Oh yes you are, Tony!" said Mandy. "And as for you, Barney White, you might think you're Mr Cool now, but you're in for a big surprise!"

Chapter 4

The Big Swimming Race

So that was how Tony found himself standing beside the pool with the other children taking part in the school's big swimming race. Alongside him was Barney White.

For once, Barney didn't look so cool. "Good luck, Tony," he said.

It sounded like he meant it. Tony was very surprised.

"Thanks," said Tony. "Same to you."

"On your marks, get set ... go!"

The children dived into the pool and began to splash their way to the other end.

Tony remembered what his coach had said: "Take your time, get your breathing going, and then start that big kick."

Tony could hear the other swimmers.

Splash! Splash! Splash!

He could hear his friends cheering from the pool side too: "Tony! Tony! Tony!"

Tony remembered his duck feet. He began to kick like he'd never kicked before!

Kick! Kick! Kick!

Suddenly his hand touched the end of the pool. The race was over. Tony looked around. His teacher and his friends were cheering and jumping up and down. He had won!

The next moment, Tony felt a hand on his arm. It was Barney White. “That was a great swim, Tony!” he said.

“Thanks, Barney,” said Tony.

“Sorry about calling you Duck Feet,” said Barney.

“That’s all right,” said Tony. “I’m rather proud of my duck feet now!”